SandCastle™
Perfect Pets

Flashy Fish

Mary Elizabeth Salzmann
AUTHOR

C.A. Nobens
ILLUSTRATOR

Consulting Editor, Diane Craig, M.A./Reading Specialist

ABDO
Publishing Company

Published by ABDO Publishing Company, 4940 Viking Drive, Edina, Minnesota 55435.

CREDITS

Edited by: Pam Price

Concept Development: Nancy Tuminelly

Cover and Interior Design and Production: Mighty Media

Photo Credits: Brand X Pictures, Comstock, Corbis Images, Regine Mahaux/Getty Images,
ullstein-Ibis Bildagentur/Peter Arnold Inc., ShutterStock

LIBRARY OF CONGRESS CATALOGING-IN-PUBLICATION DATA

Salzmann, Mary Elizabeth, 1968-
  Flashy fish / Mary Elizabeth Salzmann ; illustrated by C.A. Nobens.
     p. cm. -- (Perfect pets)
  ISBN-13: 978-1-59928-747-8
  ISBN-10: 1-59928-747-1
  1. Aquarium fishes--Juvenile literature. 2. Aquariums--Juvenile literature. I. Nobens, C. A., ill. II. Title.

  SF457.25.S25 2007
  639.34--dc22
                                    2006033250

SandCastle™ books are created by a professional team of educators, reading specialists, and content developers around five essential components—phonemic awareness, phonics, vocabulary, text comprehension, and fluency—to assist young readers as they develop reading skills and strategies and increase their general knowledge. All books are written, reviewed, and leveled for guided reading, early reading intervention, and Accelerated Reader® programs for use in shared, guided, and independent reading and writing activities to support a balanced approach to literacy instruction.

SandCastle Level: Transitional

LET US KNOW

SandCastle would like to hear your stories about reading this book. What is your favorite page? Was there something hard that you needed help with? Share the ups and downs of learning to read. We want to hear from you! To get posted on the ABDO Publishing Company Web site, send us e-mail at:

sandcastle@abdopublishing.com

FISH

Fish make interesting, beautiful pets. They have bright, shiny scales that flash as they swim around in their aquariums or fishbowls.

Alexa feeds her goldfish every day. A pinch or two of fish food is enough.

Erin has a new fish.
She will float the bag in
the aquarium for about
30 minutes before
releasing the fish to
swim with the others.

Danielle's aquarium has a lot of plants. It's good for fish to have plants to swim and hide in.

Jerry uses a net to take his fish out of the aquarium so he can clean the aquarium and change the water.

Sebastian makes sure that the filter in his aquarium is working. The filter helps keep the aquarium water clean.

A Fish Story

Jordan has a flashy
fish named Splash.
He loves to watch
Splash dart and dash.

But he thinks it would
be even more fun
if he had another one.

Jordan goes
to the fish store.
Fish tanks are stacked
from ceiling to floor!

Jordan picks out
the perfect fish,
takes her home,
and names her Splish.

Splish gets used to
her new home
before Jordan sets
her free to roam.

Jordan hopes getting
Splish wasn't wrong.
He hopes she and
Splash will get along.

When Jordan lets Splish
go into the tank,
she swims down
to the ship that sank.

Splash and Splish race
all over the place.
Jordan watches them
with a smile on his face.

Fun facts

Goldfish lose their color if they are kept in dim light.

A baby fish is called a fry.

Goldfish were first kept as pets during the Chinese Sung Dynasty, more than 1,000 years ago.

The study of fish is called ichthyology.

Scientists estimate there are between 20,000 and 40,000 species of fish. Many new fish species are discovered each year.

Glossary

filter – a device that separates floating matter from the liquid or gas that passes through it.

pinch – the amount you can hold between your thumb and one finger.

release – to set free or let go.

roam – to walk around without deciding ahead of time where you want to go.

scale – one of the small, hard pieces of skin that cover the bodies of fish, reptiles, and some mammals.

tank – a large container for fish or reptiles to live in.

About SandCastle™

A professional team of educators, reading specialists, and content developers created the SandCastle™ series to support young readers as they develop reading skills and strategies and increase their general knowledge. The SandCastle™ series has four levels that correspond to early literacy development in young children. The levels are provided to help teachers and parents select appropriate books for young readers.

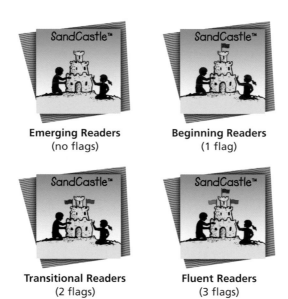

Emerging Readers
(no flags)

Beginning Readers
(1 flag)

Transitional Readers
(2 flags)

Fluent Readers
(3 flags)

These levels are meant only as a guide. All levels are subject to change.

To see a complete list of SandCastle™ books and other nonfiction titles from ABDO Publishing Company, visit **www.abdopublishing.com** or contact us at: 4940 Viking Drive, Edina, Minnesota 55435 • 1-800-800-1312 • fax: 1-952-831-1632